Pains

Text and Manuscripts: Zhao Lihong
Translator's Introduction and Translation of Poems: Karmia Chan Olutade
Afterword: Zhang Dinghao
Translation of Afterword: Xu Qin

Cover Image: Dai Weiyang
Interior Design: Xue Wenqing
Cover Design: Wang Wei

Editors: Canaan Morse, Cao Yue
Editorial Director: Zhang Yicong

Senior Consultants: Sun Yong, Wu Ying, Yang Xinci
Managing Director and Publisher: Wang Youbu

ISBN: 978-1-60220-260-3

Address any comments about *Pains* to:

Better Link Press
99 Park Ave
New York, NY 10016
USA

or

Shanghai Press and Publishing Development Company, Ltd.
F 7 Donghu Road, Shanghai, China (200031)
Email: comments_betterlinkpress@hotmail.com

Printed in China by Shenzhen Donnelley Printing Co., Ltd.
1   3   5   7   9   10   8   6   4   2

Pains

By Zhao Lihong

Translated by Karmia Chan Olutade

Better Link Press

Contents

Translator's Introduction

The wind says, your earth still lives
my breath cannot break you
                              —"Hair"

Pains is a collection of poems pulsating with the aches of a generation. The voice speaking throughout is as one rehabilitated from amnesia or intentional forgetfulness after the loss of innocence. These are a cycle of poems where a soul is reintroduced to his body, part by part, until a man is formed again by metaphor.

Zhao Lihong's career in Chinese literature spans thirty prolific years. He is one of the most successful prose writers in Mainland China, with over seventy collections in circulation and pieces taught at every level of education nationwide. His work is decorated with many of the top literary honors in China and his work frequently travels abroad. *Pains* is his second collection of poetry translated into English and the first to debut in North America.

Born in a crowded Shanghainese *longtang* residence on

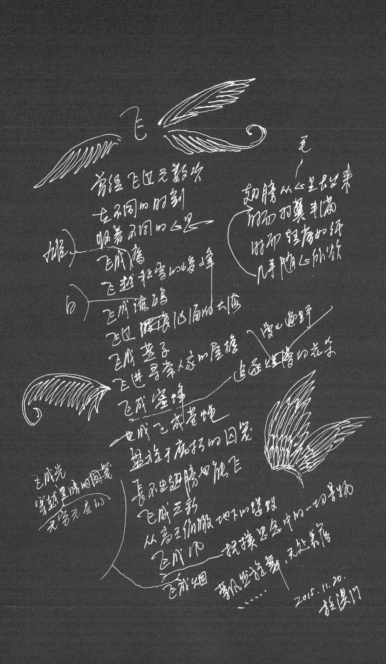

Flying, see page 71.

East Beijing Street in 1951, Zhao Lihong's mother was a doctor and his father a semi-literate, hardworking man. Zhao taught himself to read by the age of five and could recite a host of traditional Chinese literature by heart in his childhood. He fell in love with Rabindranath Tagore's *Stray Birds* in high school, but only started writing during the Down to the Countryside Movement, when he was sent to a rural island. By 1977, when colleges and universities were reinstated in China, Zhao attended East China Normal University and majored in Chinese Literature. His leadership in the Shanghai literary scene and his national influence since then cannot be understated.

The most arresting lines of his poetry are always trapdoors in the mundane. He is a simple, bread-and-butter romantic.

Touching the silk scarf before my chest
I think of silk-spitting worms on the mulberry tree
Those encased creatures
dreamt of bursting forth in flight
but were boiled for their silk instead

Listening to this tender lament
I think of the singer
The sad and lonely one
who drank down the bitter years
but wove that soured history into a rope of kindness

This moment in his poem "Association" is one such

逆旅之岁月之河

时光如风 逆向而来
拂动我鬓四百卷
往回走，往回走
看眼前离去的景色是谁

盘旋空中的飞鸟
绘之离逝挺拔
丰满的羽翼瞬间脱落
脱落成羽翼幼稚 雏鸟
扑动无毛的肉翅
咳之弱喘
鸣声未显

巢穴中几枚彩卵 巢外鸟窝
巢穴的散错头是天空 回系大树
树叶如蝴蝶 绿羽旋舞
绿叶如云烟回
枝干如车轮回转向
时间削减，又圆
云飞缩成红芽
幼芽缩成一粒种子

Going Upstream on River Time, see page 55.

example. After a lengthy, hammering list of associated thoughts that would have lulled any mind to sleep, Zhao brings in a jab from nowhere at the close of the poem that turns what would otherwise be a nursery rhyme on its head.

Or take an examination of fingerprints in the lattice of a nature poem, for instance. After examining the disappearances of his ever-evasive fingerprints, Zhao turns towards the flowers and the bugs for the answer to the question of human effervescence:

> My prints
> left too on the glassy dew
> buds in first bloom
> timid petals and gossamer grass
> the butterfly that was caught but released
> carrying my seal upon its brilliant wings
> flying the whole sky over

Zhao proves that litany is not always reserved to lifeless objects. In his categories, life teems and affected imagery, having been strained to the maximum by skepticism and irony, may just become the most unaffected choice.

Zhao Lihong's meditations on an aging body, his Songs of Experience, are not hamstrung by nostalgia, though the terms of missing are simply expressed, with childlike poetics. It is that wonder and lack of self-consciousness that sets him apart from many of his peers. Translating this slender collection was like attending a celebration of an elderly gentleman's second childhood—the gentle birth of an innocence after all the labors of the world have ceased and the debt of youth has been fully and finally paid.

Karmia Chan Olutade

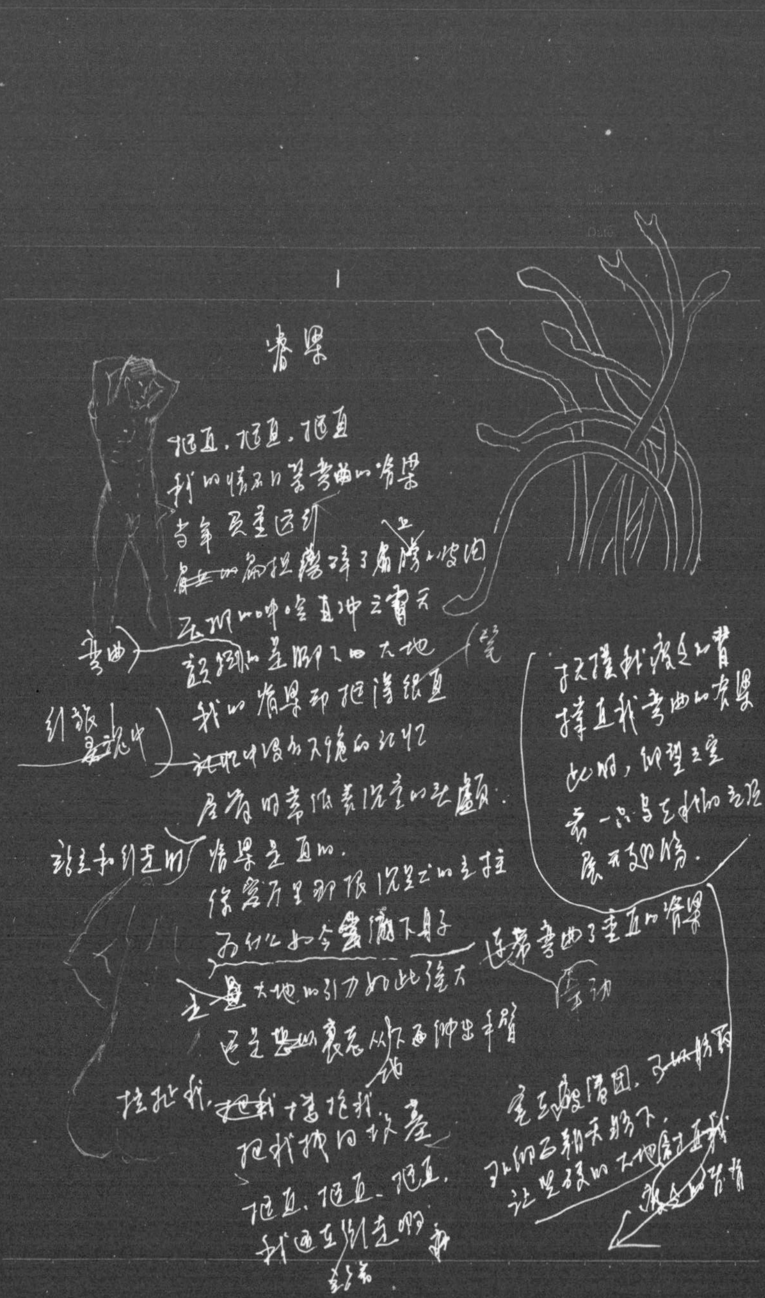

Spine, see facing page.

Spine

Straighten, straighten, straighten!
My helplessly curving spine

Back then, you carried heavy loads and traveled far
The yoke tore through the flesh of your shoulders
Your suppressed moan shot into the sky
The earth beneath me trembled, and bent
my spine stayed straight

In all my voyages, I never once knelt down
though my head was hung low from the burden
When I stood and when I walked
my spine stayed true
True as that silent pillar in the living room
true as my old father's mahogany cane

Why then, am I bent
my straight spine stooping low
Is it that the earth's gravity has overcome
or is it decay reaching up from the earth towards me
yanking me, clutching me
pulling me into the grave

Straighten, straighten, straighten
Do I not still walk upright?
If I am weary in earnest
I will lie down supine
allowing the robust land to

support my bone-tired body
and smooth my curved spine
In that moment, as I watch the sky
I see a bird above my head
flapping its wings

Straighten, straighten, straighten
my yet unbroken spine

Tongue

Tastebuds
hiding beneath the tongue
I do not know their disposition
but I rely on their sensitivity
I have tasted all of the earth's flavors

Root of tongue
connecting to the vocal cord
Every sentence I utter
Every word
Every sigh
is tied to it

I use it to lick
to taste
to kiss
use its thousands of sinews
to remain fastened to a nature
asking questions I cannot answer
It asks:

That which is born in a mouth
what is it for
Is it to taste
Is it to speak
or is it for the functions of love

The Sole and the Road

Every time I touch the land
a new road is born
My feet measure the earth
Feeling for the threshold to wonderland

The difficult mountain
the anxious water
the skinny cliff
and the clingy mire
have all torn at my soles

Each step
marks the land
The light of my life
shot somewhere away

The land gives me corns as keepsake
flowering on my heels
and the cragged cracks of my ankles

I use my sole to knock on the land and question
The road begins with my prints
but it will not stop when I do

Scars

When naked
I find scars
Great and small lacerations
Reaching all corners of my skin

I had fallen too many times
Hit, yanked
Harsh blades
Blunt bricks
Ran their course across my unguarded skin
Blood blew open as flowers
Dizzying reds
Excruciating reds
In the reds, primordial heaven and earth
then, darkness as far as eye can see

The flowers wither instantly
After the petals fall, scars form as fruit
of a wounded body
pregnant with secrets

They are worried eyes
are pains poised to permeate
In every scar
wings will be born
They will bear me up until I am a bird
combing the streams of lost time
to find life young again

Soul Departs

The soul and the body sometimes part
the former creeps out of its shell
It vaults from flesh and wanders on air
but does not win its freedom
The wandering soul
misses the body it once possessed
but there is no homecoming

Transmute into a bird
alight on the branch
and watch hurried pedestrians

I am the soul perched on that tree
curiously watching someone below
inhabiting my body
Running, dancing
Looking about among the throng
Lost in thought in my room
…
I on the tree, I on the ground
are closer than breath
but worlds apart
My soul does not know
what my flesh is brooding
and I don't know where to go
My flesh raises his head to look up
but cannot see my soul
A few dry leaves tremble in the wind

Where am I now
Where am I

The departed soul
can become a mirror
to reveal the body

I am the shining one
My soul
stands waiting before
my flesh
The specter in the mirror
flashes phosphorescent
A terrified face comes
Someone I do not know
A faded trench coat
Toes showing from a pair of leather shoes
Pushing a pile of luggage forever closed
…
Or maybe he doesn't see a thing
The mirror is empty
A stranger looks in
Suddenly helpless
Speechless
Where am I now
Where am I

Hair

My hair
used to be raven wisps, soft
sunlit waterfall. A refraction
of the rainbow at sky's edge
wild grasses, boiling in the wind
saluting the earth with wild dance

Color, stored up
Life and all its hues
Black, bid daylight goodbye
and commissioned to chase dawn, ever behind
Black hair grows, the process
renders all lengths
short

When did it happen
black becoming white?
White as smoke ash, white as surviving snow
White, rough, vacuous
A sigh that cuts through glacier

Those remnant threads
on my head
thinning by the day
when the wind comes, they still float
The wind says, your earth still lives
my breath cannot break you

Prints

I leave upon the world
my meandering footprints
and more: translucent fingerprints
on everything I felt
I leave behind as a secret trail

Mother's breast
Father's shoulder
Lover's cheek
Son's small hand
Cotton jacket, sackcloth, silk
The coat flapping in the winter wind
and the rain-soaked hat brim

Chopsticks, goblets, teapots
ink and brushes, book pages, abacus
flute-holes, flag poles, piano ivory
a winding banister
the handle of a forgotten umbrella, a crutch
all manners of keys
innumerable door handles
…

Rice cake, berry, leafy greens
I grind them all
down until my prints are erased altogether
I save them
then destroy them

The prints go through my esophagus
into my hungry gut
They return to partake in me

My prints
left too on the glassy dew
buds in first bloom
timid petals and gossamer grass
the butterfly that was caught but released
carrying my seal upon its brilliant wings
flying the whole sky over

Overlap

Worlds forever overlapping
Over and under
Over and under

Look outside
There are windows beyond this window
Doors beyond this door
Mountains beyond this mountain
Skies beyond this sky

Look inside
A pupil within my pupil
Mouth within my mouth
Heart within my heart
Soul within my soul

How to break away from this overlap
breaking off the lock of layers
First, go inland
Then, come out

Open wide that pupil within
Ignite that internal heart
Set off that soul within this soul
Push out that window beyond
Open that door yonder
Ascend the mountain higher
Regard the sky

That world without overlap
where all roads go wide
just may be a free one

Nails

I won't investigate
how many claw marks and where
I won't find
how those places have changed from my scratches
I only wonder
why the countless cuttings
have never stopped them from growing
Grass of the field, leaf from the branch
like my everlasting black hair
Silk in the impenetrable
Gentility in the rough

If in this life they were never cut
what would they have become
I'd be the hermit
They'd be vines
wrapped around my hands and feet
binding me in an unknown corner
The world would be covered by my nails
eclipsing the sun
...

If I travel
they wouldn't become such manacles
or hindrances of the journey
The thorns and ivies
climbing stones and cliffs
would file them down

Scratch marks and nail powder
left behind in all places left behind
…

Still I must
kiss them with the clipper
occasionally admiring
their pared stature
Pruning
is the price of civilization, the consequence
of our ancestors abandoning the forest

The Color of Dreams

Dreamscapes dissipate
All that is remembered
are the vibrant specks, the shards

Sometimes my dreams are technicolored
more fresh and raw
than the real world
Other dreams are in black and white
as the dusty old films
a century ago

In the dreams of color
I float, I dance on air
Twilight and the budding clouds
accompany me as wings
a tornado of color
Music and fragrance
engulf me
like wine
From that misty outlook
The world has thousands of pustules
Each orifice
oozes blinding hues
…

In the dreams of black and white
I run, I struggle
Cliffs and deathly gorges

surround me
Along with harrowing torrents and undercurrents
and the dead who visit
who sit before me and do not speak
in the silence of the black and white
When I awake, I am exhausted
tears hang by the frame of my eyes
and all that I can touch
momentarily loses color too
…

But I would never know
where, in dream, the bliss and sorrows
well up from
Colored dreams and monochrome
sometimes go to war
hemming me in the middle
In that dreamscape
there is only a primeval gray

Premonition

Lightning cleaves the nightmare
I open my eyes
Morning light quivers in the window

The fragments of dream
are petals dispersing
speckled butterflies
weightless wind

My pupils are pleased
for but a moment
when suddenly I am met
by a feline's steady gaze
The cat on the roof is looking down on me
green eyes burning like two planets

A flying body suddenly plummets
Solitary lightning
Still frame

Vocal Cords

My vocal cords sounded
true as a tuned string
that held up the music
of dripping dew

I once thought that vocal cords were for singing
Any breath from the earth
Could hum them
Anyone could be a composer
The cords chase after a heavenly tune
from which all harmonies are derived

But there are moments of stillness
in the cacophony of the globe
My cords turn hoarse
My own voice
imprisoned, invisible
deceivingly close

Death spreads a net of silence around me
My cords cannot help but shake
and scream until my heart and lungs are rent
the sound thundering until it tears asunder
this taciturn world
that allows no echoes

Lacrimal Gland

A mysterious secretion
turns emotion into liquid
Time and again
my eyes flood

Agony and joy
assemble as crystals
crowding my pupils
blurring my sight

Charging sandstorms
Chest-piercing bullets
and those sudden
departures, those deathbeds
trained my tear ducts

My tears have long evaporated into air
but the glands do not quit
the tracks of tear drops
radiate out like the veins of a plant
gathering the potsherd of remembrance
to reconstruct
an eternal begonia leaf

Relics

One after the other my dear ones
depart from me
Warm bodies chill
are scorched into smoke
dissolving in midair

They leave me
a few papers
a swatch of knitting
an empty box
These reticent relics
long since lost the warmth of their master's touch
calm and solemn
examine my memories

The papers bear the markings of the dead
beneath a tearful gaze
the words move
They emit a gentle, familiar sound
and drag me back in time
to sit beneath the moon
walk through fields
sail on the seas
sojourn in a foreign land
…

Then, the frigid relics
recover their warmth
the knitted things fashion themselves into flying rugs
carrying me over the river of years
upstream against the currents
the empty box
instantly glistens with pearls and precious stones
and I am rapt through tears

Expectations

I wait in expectation
for the extinguished lamp to flare up again
The sound of turning metal
comes from the friendless keyhole
Low-hanging curtains move in the wind
on the strange staircase
a familiar shadow flashes by
...

I wait in expectation
What exorcizes the darkness
is not the abrasive car horn
nor hoarse human breathing
nor the shriek of the alarm
but the crow of the rooster
innocent, clear
as a newborn's crying
summoning a blood red sunset
petals scattered into the sky
...

I had no more patience
for what I hoped for
Alone, I heard
the bird's dirge
But by the time I looked up
the sky bore
not a hint of wings

Association

Clutching the pencil in my hand
I think of the tree that birthed it
Its wood must still
remember the forest
the buzz of life within it

Drinking a savory soup
I think of the salt melted by the broth
Those grains
must still remember the sea
vicious waves, schools of free fish

Ten thousand ways for ice to flower on glass
I think of the north wind that howled all night
In the darkness it rode out to earth's end
never thinking that its brutish trail
would leave such delicate footprints

Watching a distant kite sashay in the sky
I think of children running on the earth
The child who cheers for his own kite
will never know that the brittle line in his hands
tugs an old man back to his childhood

Touching the silk scarf before my chest
I think of silk-spitting worms on the mulberry tree
Those encased creatures
dreamt of bursting forth in flight
but were boiled for their silk instead

Listening to this tender lament
I think of the singer
The sad and lonely one
who drank down the bitter years
but wove that soured history into a rope of kindness

Eardrum

Ears are just embellishments
Whether they are elephantine in the breeze
or dainty as copper coins
the lobes are meant to make a distinction
as foil for the face

The most magical of all is the eardrum
It hides
a prisoner in a great hall
never to see the sun
but somehow sensing the breath
of all that lives between heaven and earth

The eardrum trembles
from surrounding sounds
the thunderstorm's bellows
the hum of mosquitoes, flies
the song of a nightingale
the toad's throaty drum
and the mass of humankind
No matter the distance
they reach my eardrums
and fully resound

My eardrums neighbor the brain
It trembles as they do
They even connect to
the distant heart

When the eardrums tremble
the heart hastens
for all the sounds of the earth
prophesy
and carry the heart

The same voice
in different eardrums
reverberates differently
Some smile ear to ear
while others cry
No one knows
the difference

Eyes

The gusts of time
have blown off my last eyelashes
My eyes are defenseless

Facing the leviathan of time
I open eyes without lashes
Beneath the force of my gaze, time
opens its garments
I see the long scar across its body
and that unfathomable cavern

In the dimness
shimmers the light of a silver skeleton
A moth, appalled, flies out from the crevice
wings stirring a wind
straight for my eyes

Eternity

Every moment
is an unreturning eternity
Every eye met
every shoulder brushed
every unintended stay
every blind dash
every muted tear
every passing smile
is eternal
is eternal

You want to catch
the light and sound around you
But that sudden vision
departs upon arrival
With every flash of lightning
every wisp of wind
every exhalation
every measure of chimes
every bout of birds soaring by
every session of click and slam, doors, windows
is eternal
is eternal

Visiting the Dead in Dreams

1

Father, who passed over twenty years ago
suddenly appears in my dreams
Without notice or knock on the door
he stood quietly before me
smiling as he did then
only his eyes were sad
Awestruck, I cried out
but my mouth produced no sound
I reached for Father
he retreated, smiling

In my memories
Father never showed anger
Even his despair and sadness
were soft as mist
Who says dreams quarrel with reality?
Father, who visited my dream
regarded me with his old smile
I want this moment to freeze
A honk from outside the window
jolts me mercilessly

2

I have never been frightened
of the dead who visit in dreamland
They often come uninvited
and momentarily I am unsure
of the border between living and the dead
Conversation with them is hard
Relationship harder
They are silent black and white films
rolling in the serendipitous dark

Days spent in bitter remembrance of the departed
don't bring them back in dreams
I pray wordlessly before I sleep
Come, come visit me
I want to see you
The dream door creaks open
but I am not the one who enters
Out come faces I have never met:
characters from books
celebrities I know by name
then long-sleeved ancients
then suited and tuxedoed foreigners

3

The first hours of one endless dream
were misted
the latter half as sharp as shadows in moonlight
A boy dressed in his underwear
walks toward me
his black eyes sparkling
his skeletal frame shining
Atop his head, a spinning halo of flying insects
They trail him like a buzzing kite
He walks past and looks sidelong at me
From his black eyes
two crystal teardrops. Unmistakably
his quivering lips ask
Do you still know me

Of course, I recognize you
Memories come mid-dream
dream within the dream
Truth flies over space-time
I return to the summer day
you lay in the marsh by the bank
The river had just swallowed your young life
The afternoon sun shone upon your naked body
You and I were the same age
but you were the one who showed me death
That spirit casually took your hand in the water
made you into a corpse no one claimed
and drew crowds beneath the sun
A fly landed on your eyelashes
You did not blink

4
What is a dream
a track not taken
another stage
of twisted reality
the microscopic magnified for a second
a mysterious hint
a rehearsal of fate
the curse of the ancients
temptation on the horizon
or is it the quick lightning
when death and life crash at midnight

I too have dreamt of Hades
that faceless shadow
who casts out his black net from the dark
casting a spark in the gloom
a distant quivering fire
a garden full of open cherry blooms
a luxurious, exotic scent hovering
a long-nailed hand
suddenly waving at you
and a blazing chariot
carries you, volleys you into the abyss

Bamboo Flute

I am a bamboo flute
with eight holes
pregnant with incalculable notes
My previous life
was spent in the wild valley
where I let streams
mirror my green as I swayed in the wind

I await your lips
your tender yet excited breath
to enter my body
come now, pads of fingers
come feel each of my keys
as if a bee seeking stamen

Your breath
paces the length of me
striking each cavernous hole
until it sprouts a new leaf
a bud
a thread of perfume
a tear

And now, it is as if I have been remade
returned to that shy bamboo
surrounded by wind
gingerly
waving, dancing, moaning
...

Lungs

My lungs are leaves that fan
as breath moves out and in
Air of this world
formless and formed
once flirtatious and grave
once madly rambunctious
emitting echoes that move the soul

When I was young, my lungs
were green saplings
despite growing up hard
starved and alone
they breathed
fresh air

I never learned to smoke
and so my lungs were spared
from the harms of nicotine

Now that my sideburns are frosty white
and I no longer worry about my livelihood
my lungs are shrouded by smog
How can a flimsy mask
keep out such
penetrating dust

My Shadow

If you ask
who is the most faithful friend
my answer is
my shadow

My shadow forever follows me
for richer or poorer
in grief and jubilation
in lavish places
or the barren wilderness
No matter where I go
my shadow is perpetually fastened to my feet
Steadfast

They say that the difference between the quick and the dead
is whether the body stands over its shadow
The living have shadows
Ghosts are alone
As for what my shadow looks like
I cannot say
Sometimes he can become a giant
highlighting my minuscule frame
Other times he can become as small
as the outline of my shoe soles

When I walk away from the light
my shadow walks before me
When I run towards the light

my shadow goes missing
When I search in the darkness
it escapes me
but when even a ray of light is found
then I have recovered it

Yes, it is also the one
I know the least
My shadow
do you feel sadness
Do you ponder
Do you smile with me
Do you weep
It holds its tongue
Rendering me speechless

If this world cannot tell the living from the dead
I give thanks for shadows
I would avoid ghosts
and only befriend the shadowed man
and my shadow too would, in his bashfulness
surface from my vanity to remind me
You are a man alive
You ought to live as such

Beam of Light

Into a house without doors or windows
dives a beam of light
cleaving the darkness
shining into the inky void

Hello, light
Your clarity
grants the formless air substance
You hang perpendicular
like a glaringly pure pillar
a burning crystal
or the winter ice
Do you lead to freedom
to a sky where wings unfold

You sparkle silently
as if to say:
why don't you try
to take hold and climb me
go along down me to escape your gloom
Freedom and imprisonment
are only separated by a thin metal sheet

I extend my hand
into the empty beam
a bloodless palm
ignites a full red
The remaining blood

flowing in a vermillion translucence
melding into the light itself

That cold light that cannot be grasped
suddenly becomes warm
as if an electric current zapped through my being
Hello, light
Please lead me out of my sealed house
to embrace the outside world

I close my eyes
bearing up weightless light
Darkness breaks with a clattering sound
That sound becomes
ten thousand more beams of light
as if made of all the lightning in the world
from every direction shooting towards me
through the worldly dimness
silently, it comes, but glorious

In the quiet
I become a beam of light

Going Upstream on River Time

Time rushes backwards
past my gray hairs
I return, I return
the scenery spins

The birds flying circles above
fall into the canopy
Their plush plume disassemble
and beneath it, their yellow baby fur reemerge
They flap their furless wing stubs
and cry out for food
Their cry does not end
before they disappear into a few blushing eggs
and lie quietly in woven nests

The nest comes apart. Twigs and fallen leaves
circle around the tree
like dancing butterflies, like green tongues
they shrink back into the branches
The branches are taken into the trunk
like arms, as the trunk sinks in earth
The crown of the tree loses its green
and the tree returns to a sapling
the sapling becoming a seed
borne by the wind

The seed is picked up
by a pedestrian

Those other hurried pedestrians
all become magicians
The elderly become raven-haired
their wrinkles vanishing like lightning
Their bumbling steps lighten
Old men become young bucks
Old women become maidens
Youngsters turn into infants
Their crying shatters the world
and jars it from reverie

The nightmare is a science fiction blockbuster
melting ancient glaciers into pulsating springs
pushing the jade fields into a mighty open sea
The waves toss and turn towards sky's end
The dried-up ocean floor looms upwards, becoming mountain peaks
and mountains fissure and break down into a wilderness plain
The plain slides beneath a violent tide
The tide slowly laps up the endless forest
The forest sighs itself into cascading grass
and in the grass a small creek flows
In that creek a fish swims towards me
The fish says: I am your forefather

Metamorphosis

Time and again
I am murdered
in my poetry
in words I have willfully scattered
From the road I came
picked up my words
I can no longer recover the old scent
from pieces of the early silt
My voice belongs to neither
the confident oath-taker
nor the nervous reckoner
Dimple, tear sparkle, sigh:
only an indistinct scar left
…

I am like a drowned man
in the thick of a dark flow
struggling, spastic, suffocated
my arm reaching out of the water
like a broken branch scurried downstream
I hear my own screams
ripping my heart and lungs
but I am silent
…

When the branches wash to shore
and whirlpools pass away one by one
green sprouts erupt

from a face full of wrinkles
I look back expecting
a torrent heading my way
but see only a blue fire
encamped around the glacier
I watch the black night escort the dawn
hear the spring wind trail the cold winter
Silence, silence, silence
…

When the whole world explodes into view again
I have already become a toddler
I face the turbulent clear flow
my bags completely empty
All that was carefully stored away
is abandoned now
Go back to the guileless years then
Let me survey at the world anew
Let the world recognize me slowly

The Arrow of Time

It shoots unstoppably through
the dark of nought
A whistling rides through
Silence
A rushing chases
stagnation

The heavens and the earth
are pierced
glaciers become water
forests reduced to nurseries
All the vanity of humanity
obliterated to pieces
strewn about the sky
leaves that fall after an autumn wind

Sound rushes by my ears
Specks of light fly
coming from the distance
When it reaches my eyes
I think I can catch them as prey
but they flash by
and become wintry stars on the horizon

Pains

No need for points and blades
or bats and sticks to hit with
Those painful instants split
like lightning at night
and drive straight into the heart
Yet, no blood is shed
You will not find the hairline scar
I can't tell you where the hurt is
how it subsumes every inch of me
from my open face
to my hidden frame
…

Sometimes, a cool breeze alone
could recall the pain
Or a pair of questioning eyes
burn like a searing rod
and even a second question
can be briars across the back
…

I am harassed by pain, frequently
but I am not afraid
The living are weak
Numbness is a greater tragedy
If I were catatonic
I may as well be a withered branch
a cold cliff rock

Even silvergrass
cries, broken by a mad wind
Even reed
wails, trampled by the storm

Trespassing

Fish swim around the ceiling
Kites polka in the bathtub
Sailboats advance on the hillside
Snowflakes dance in the fire
Above a colorful marriage bed
hear the howl of a Tibetan mastiff
From an infant's crib
swings a pair of old reading glasses
The mouse dashes into the cat's bed
and the sparrow occupies the eagle's nest
...

Indecent occupation
cannot last forever
Even with ten thousand keys
you cannot open
a door that is not yours
Should you try the window
you would find no floor below
Floorboards become a mat of needles
ready to pierce any unprepared sole
Jump then, and run
Wear yourself out
...

A bamboo basket cannot hold water
A net cannot hold wind
A foreign gaze
will never pierce
the guards around my heart

Transplanting

Grab the stem
pull the roots
from their first den
put it in strange soil

Transplant the ancient kernel
into the modern mind
Lush sprays grow
over and over
wondrously
like the bodhisattva's thousand hands
the bat's ten thousand pairs of wings
extending and waving in the sky

The desires of men
burst open as imaginary flowers
with dark stamens
and crystalline petals
The fragrance is laced with a mysterious air
a rotting perfume
the sweet fume of hard labor
the aroma of millennia under the yoke
explode
in the world of sense

Falling ashes
A flower blooms late
its face a human face
the cunning smile
invites the flowers and the bees
where no feathers land

Only a sigh
Ah, you aren't
You aren't the flower of the day

Piano Keys

When I meditate
with my palms pressed against my chest
I touch my ribs
with my own fingers

They become piano keys
returning my press
My right hand hops along my left ribs
My left hand charges across my right
There is no melody to track
but I drum along, playing
the sonata that belongs to me

Heartbeat and breath
complement the rhythm of the ribs
My organs resonate
Hear my lungs inflate
Witness the fidelity of my organs
Mine are not adept fingers
and the ribs within me quaver
I play music
I alone can hear

Fearful trembling
Momentary suffocation
An unnamed pang
A hungry wheeze
All these notes of joy and suffering

are encased beneath my ribs
The sands of time
cannot bury them

The dream of being a musician
is a submarine in my heart
Longing fingers
feel along the keys
Before my eyes, a world of black and white

I Want to Forget

I want to forget
the night I got hurt
blood and chips of moonlight
adhere to memory's nerves
and I ache

I want to forget
that flash flood
the sirens over the rapids
slowly freezing
I am a film still in the rush of water
A note without sound

I want to forget
the voice that intoxicated me
But the clock falls, continues to fall
and time moves on like a bow across a string
Shaking every inch
that I displace

Where Dawn and Dusk Meet

Dawn and night
happen upon each other
The first rooster to crow breaks the solace
A thin thread of light pierces the black veil
The morning star shines
and in the lake of night, a ripple fans out

The dream shorts out
Light returns to its source
The cacti shake in the wind
The shattered dream is an opening shell
and night is hidden in it
pearly tears glistening

Darkness once blackened the world
It also established the want of light
We imagined, presupposed light
that could incinerate what stood between earth and sky
light and dark
equally long

Light, appears at the sky's edge
Unhurried
Unpredictable
All the colors in the air
parade out one by one from its touch
What is left behind is only darkness

Yet darkness lives on
It lives in the light that fills the space between
If you don't believe me
just close your eyes

Flying

Countless times, I have flown
in different circumstances
carrying different emotions
Wings grew from my heart
whenever they wanted
Sometimes feathers grew thick
other times, they were thin, paper-like

I flew as an eagle
over snowy peaks and tundra
the earth unrolled beneath me
I flew as a seagull
over roiling waves
the tide shook my young soul
I flew as a swallow
landing on eaves ringed with hearth smoke
enjoying human warmth
I flew as a bee
in pursuit of flowering hillside
tasting nature's honeyed fragrances
I have flown too, as a fly
circling the rusted cage
high off the fumes of filth

The wingless can still take flight
Fly as clouds
watching the ant-like civilizations below
Fly as the wind
to caress every imagined place and thing
Fly as smoke
waltzing
unable to land

...

Thinking of Death

Thinking of death
everything tranquil before me
One flower white
blooming zealously in the dark
One flower black
opening in white
There is no time to review life's journey
memories like asteroids
blaze by
astounding and short-lived
In the ravine of my ears rush human voices
tumbling thick as a snowstorm
falling and lonely in the gray
then splendid in the sun
Melting
Melting
Disappearing without proof
without exception
melting into the cracked earth

Thinking of death
an unknowable sweetness wells up in my heart
The tastes of the past
no matter how bitter, soured
or spiced with resentment
will pass
and yesterday and the future
mingle before my eyes

until they are indistinguishable
Life is a spinning plate
spinning
and spinning
and spinning past clouds, sun, rain, snow
past barbed wire and fetters
past smog and fault lines
past the forced laughter in the great hall
the great squire and the prison cell
Now, it spins towards
total freedom

Thinking of death
I feel an odd longing
Those birth beds and deathbeds
will become history
Those departed ones I loved
will turn their heads to wait for me
and in the cosmos, innumerable strings hang

invisible
connected to everything I miss
What strings I thought were cut
and disintegrated to ashes
are now reconnecting
Closure and rebirth
fellowship here
and perhaps this is life
an utterly altered beginning

Clouds scatter
Starlight lands with a splash
Lights dim
Curtains fall
Flower black and flower white
open at the same time
in darkness
in light

Losing My Way

I've lost my way, I'm lost
Why can't I find my way home
I've lost my way, I'm lost
…

In my dreams I hear Father calling
again and again, anxious and afraid
I awake to find myself in a cemetery
forested by gravestones
The graves are all similarly
granite and square
like fallen dominoes
speechless, resigned
that first push long gone
…

The pine planted that year
now reaches my brow
Just as tall as Father stood
The pine sways in the wind
every needle
holds a drop of dew
endless jewels for tears
…

Starlight visits every night
The night wind beats
every sealed stone gate
Those who pace the place
like black or white pieces
treading the checkered game board
The paths are narrow, and very straight
but you still lose your way

…

Where are you, Father
you must not like your cramped stone room
You would not enjoy the damp darkness
and so have come out to wander
When I lost my way as a child
you were always the one to find me
How could you be lost

…

In life, you were imprisoned in a small room
You said, in the next life you wanted space
You had become smoke
wandering through the air
but in the end, you were returned to this place
a room narrower than the one you lived in
accompanied by countless strangers

...

I'm lost, lost
Father's voice comes close and then drifts away
I'm lost, lost
the cemetery is wide and deep
no way of exiting this dream
though I wake and wake
icy tears printed onto my pillow

...

Storm

Within inches
almost within touch
but I have never
held your hand
I have called after you in my mind
in thin sighs
in thundering interjections
like boulders in a mudslide
You were always so close
and unreachable
clearly present one second
then nowhere to be found

From one end of the sky to another
sometimes my cries are returned by your
intermittent breathing
and your heartbeat
like raindrops pattering on the grass
or birds scalping clouds
…
So infinitesimal, the sounds
but unmistakable to me

Thoughts of you sit still
in my universe of one
they congregate, a storm-in-waiting

Diving

I often fantasize
of life as a fish
This is a vision with a reason
My ancestor's ancestor's ancestor's
ancestor's ancestor's ancestor's
ancestor...
was once a fish

Swimming down
enveloped by the white waters
The cool and the clear
currents move about me
I stir the water
it massages me
My limbs are fins
My feet are tails, rudders
I open wide my eyes
to find the dappled sunlight refracting
The goal is in sight, beyond the muck

It is just that I dare not breathe
dare not open my mouth
I am bloated from holding my breath
so full I could rocket into the sky
My wish is to be a flying fish
but I fall back down into the waves
heavy and dumb
water splashing up over my head
My limbs flail
but are obstructed by the torrent
from embracing
my ancestor's ancestor's ancestor's
ancestor's ancestor's ancestor's
ancestor...

Walking into Three Spaces at Once

I bring my feet over the threshold
and walk into three spaces at once

My body enters one
surrounded by everything tangible:
the boards on the floor
the painting framed on the wall
the swinging chandelier from the ceiling
the smell of paint in the air
…

Yet, my soul enters a different plane
one belonging to passed time
blurred expressions
faraway echoes
all that happened behind the door
all the living and dying
…

My mind enters into a third space
belonging to a future mystery
bramble of light and shadows
hides an unknown voyeur
Every corner conceals
a miracle waiting to explode
…

I walk through a door
and sense three different spaces
The material atmosphere shifts inside my body
My soul shifts freely in the revelry
A tiny room
becomes deep space

...

The Written Word

After a getting by for so long
we are the closest of friends
the most distant strangers

I mutter about you
You cross before me in clusters
like soldiers before a general
or chestnuts counted by a farmer
or naive children
investigating a host of stars

You are silk strands in every color forming
a vibrant brocade
and a tangled ball of twine
twisted into a labyrinth
scattered across the wilderness
You are the liberated vagabond
crouching in dictionaries
like assassins

The same faces
can evolve
infinite expressions
You are a plate of scattered sand
yet you can consolidate the years
You are a field of broken soldiers
yet you can be built into a boulevard
that leads to a vaster, distant place
or a darkness with no end

Where I Went in Dream

A dream is like a uterus
pregnant with an inscrutable fetus
whose face always changes

As I dream of a desolate island
where tides smash the rocks
They become forests and buildings
Neon lights flicker
Lightning gathers, netting night's canvas
asteroids turn into frost flowers on glass

I dream of the kingdom of heaven
Angels floating in air
transform into black moths
Their wings covering stars and moon
A dark cloud rolls
a hot sun in its pocket

Dreaming is like riding the subway
beginning from a point of light
going through a long darkness
entering into a bright station
and what comes after
is another endless dark
…

When I wake
the heavenly lights move before me
in my ears
an piercing interrogator
Where did you go in your dream
And why
I never can reply

Door

On the road I meet
One closed door after another
Sometimes, with a slight push
they fly open
Other times, I pound and pound
and the door only opens a sliver
Some doors need no knocking to open
My footfall is the key
Other doors are locked and then locked again
sealed off like a thousand year old fortress

The invisible threshold
is a tripwire beneath my feet
Sometimes it lets me pass
Other times it triggers a deadly fall
crashing into the doorframe
A voice would say from within the door
Come inside
If it is dark outside
there may be light inside
If there is a storm outside
there may be a clear sky within

So again
I stand by the door
The door asks
do you dare enter
the world within the door
could be heaven
could be hell

Cold

A word leaves the mouth
and becomes a snowflake
flurrying within silence
The air I breathe out
condenses into fog
breaking in the winter wind
tears become ice
and vision blurs
Before glare that cuts to the bone

The cold air like knives, like needles
slices through coat, jacket, sweater, shirt
cuts into shivering skin
Even if I set myself afire
the flames would freeze
into cherry red popsicles

Observing

Formless light
shoots from different pupils
converging on one point
without luminosity or sound
they have startling power

When stony cold
like a frozen wind
they will frost the blood
When scalding hot
it can turn indifference
into hot lava
a cauldron of fire

Focused from all over
it can pierce through walls of iron
leaving the observed
no place to hide

X-Ray

An invisible beam
trespasses skin
crosses bone
climbs every artery
investigates every nerve

One can only hear the slight sound
like God knocking on a door
light's fingerprint
Light's touch
saturates my body and soul

A transparent negative
before a light shows
the secrets of flesh and spirit
blacks and whites
coalesce in mottled shadow

I open my eyes wide
allow my pupils to melt into the negative
but I can't see past this monochrome world
squirming organs are frozen
Warm blood has coalesced

The doctor says
This is your truest portrait

The Cellphone and the Network

Every pedestrian busying the boulevard
clutches a cellphone in one hand
Young girls and old ladies
are all talking into their phones
Even children have joined this tireless army
Some are flirting, others holding forth
Some speak secretively in hushed tones
They all seem to be speaking to themselves
On the other end must be
an equally ardent conversationalist

I stand on the corner imagining
the connected phones bound
by a physical line
What would the world look like
Billions of wires thrown into the air
some a few hundred meters
others tens of thousands
They crisscross and entangle in the sky
knitting an unbearably large net
that covers city and village
shades the entire earth

This net is colorful
Since every line has its own tone
Every conversation a different hue
Pink, for the amorous fussing of romance
Light blue, for the blowouts of youth
Yellow, for bored parents' endless nagging
Beige, for the elderly's resigned complaints
Gray, for bargaining and bartering
Black, for the politicians' deluding
The planet before me
would be a colossal, vibrant net

Facing such an imaginary net
I continue my fantasy
If at a certain unforeseeable moment
the world were to suddenly lose power
and all the cellphone signals were to vanish
the masses clutching cellphones
how they would yelp and cry
Disappointed, anxious and helpless expressions
would bloom like flowers all over the land
and the net that had blocked out the sun
would be gone without a trace

I ache for
the quiet after that apocalyptic devastation
The world may return to its original state
The giant net
would rest quietly upon the land
dissolved by the thoughts of humanity
What cannot be severed
though ten thousand miles apart
would still hold together
What should be cut for good
will be worlds apart
no matter how close they are

Bugs Loving on the Road

Two little black beetles
fly out from the grass and bushes
meet on the open concrete
fold away their wings
and begin a love dance

Here, where no ant or worm could disturb them
no fallen leaves of flower stems to trip on
What a flat love bed
Passion oppressed in the grass suddenly erupts
as if they had hidden a lifetime's worth of lust

Wings bat wings
antennae tangle in antennae
Shivering, shaking, turning
bodies twist into each other, inseparable
The wind bears up their joyous cries
the sound of their impassioned moaning

Then, a large tractor
approaches, thrumming
its thick wheels grinding the road as it rolls
The two little love bugs
still lost in their tryst
are utterly unaware of impending disaster

…

Living

Dreams are empty
I want to live sturdily
standing on uneven land
a dusty sky above me
I open my eyes
to see a rusted ceiling
and curtains blown in the wind

To live is to
hear the sound of running water
rain in the sky
rivers below
the kitchen faucet
a gush in the bathroom

To live, is to
suffer, to itch, to fall ill
to hunger, to thirst, to refuse food
to never get sick of the same bland congee and rice
but to also want fresh
and famous but untried flavors

To live is
to laugh, to shed tears
to yell, to sing, to stay quiet
to softly ask
in uncertain times
why

To live is to
think of those few familiar names
to see the beloved's face
to hear a shout outside the window
and to pray for another
even as they lift you up

To live is to
call my aging mother
and tell her, I will, as always
wade across the sea of city people
and sit with her, chat
and drink the black tea she pours

To live is to
remember what I ought to do tomorrow
and then to embrace my pillow
Of course I will dream
and in the dream I can ascend to heaven, descend into the
earth
but when I awake, I wash my face
with reality

My Chair

The wooden concaves and bulges, the fine lines quiet
the chair back silently massaging my spine
In front of me is a computer
Modernity flickers on the screen
Electric currents carry the hedonists
Words twirl and fly in endless transformation
…

I turn off the computer and turn
to touch the wooden grains of my chair back
suddenly feeling a cool wind meet my face
The seat becomes a tree trunk
The chair back sprouts new saplings
green vines twisting around, leaves pouring forth
Such a common wooden chair
swiftly becomes a skybound tree
capturing me beneath its canopy
…

Around my fingers, numbed by computer keys
a ring, a second, then a third appears
ancient tree rings
My body shrinks in its growth
but my heart is nurtured by the green
warmed until it is a free bird
flapping, parting its beak to sing
It flies far to the mythical mountains

Pain Is the Keystone

Joy is the outer shell
Pain is the essence

Joy is mist and ocean spray
Pain is the river that fills full

Looking for joy through pain
is like going into the field after harvest
to glean the chaff

Looking for joy through pain
is like going through a snow covered canyon
looking for flowers

It's time to learn to hammer it deep
using pain as the keystone

To ram and ram the pain down in my heart like packed dirt
deeper, deeper

Yes, pain is the keystone
On it are built mansions of joy

Dark Matter

1
every inch of space
flies with invisible spirits
guiding me, obstructing me
hitting me, enfolding me
praising me, mocking me
but I have no feeling

2
walking away from the light
light takes on mass
propelling me forward
I'll never catch up
yet I can feel
its magical push

3
folding its wings in midair
a body falls like an arrow
drops downward
is it towards an unforgiving rock
or the soft surface of a lake

4

when the target turns fuzzy
and yet you cannot stop
running
the eyes beg the ears
to read the inbound wind
the wind says: watch your step
the earth is full of invisible fault lines

5

you hide in anonymity
Do you fabricate
a lie that will never be fulfilled
or are you lying in wait
to turn the world upside down

6

shooting stars cross the night sky
burn for a moment
is it a living spirit escaping a black hole
or being drawn in

7

there is no color deeper than black
all of the colors and lights
are drowned in it
and no matter what you think
you cannot dilute it

8

when in meditation
there are silent screams
noise of explosions penetrates walls
but the sounds are stopped
by a mute overcoat
and under the clothes, a boiling heart
that refuses to be heard by anyone

9

I cannot see through this world
the world cannot see through me
x-rays can shoot through skin and bone
gamma rays can cut into organs
but cannot catch
the free mind
wandering between the heavens and the earth

10

a desperate wave
grasps at nothing
you will find no handhold there
the wind is as a fast knife
slicing through ten fingers

11

the world closes its eyes
night descends
the weary fall asleep
someone is thoughtful
birds are flying
countless pupils dilate in darkness
patiently waiting
for the world to wake

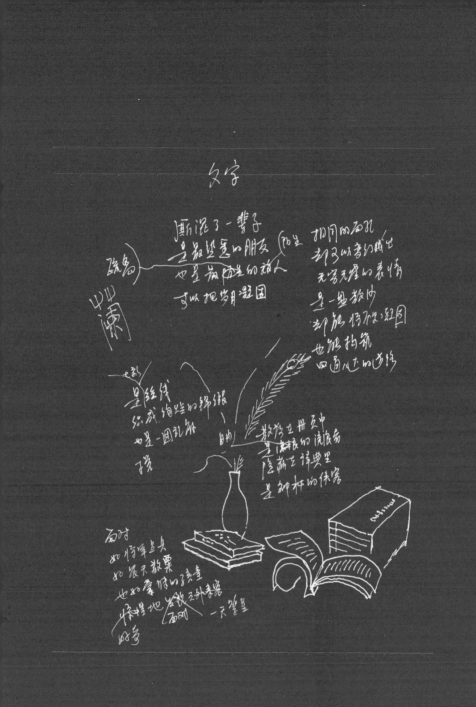

The Written Word, see page 84.

Afterword   Pains and Light

Shanghai poet Zhao Lihong is an important and one of the most influential poets in contemporary China. He started writing poetry in his youth and has worked quietly and determinedly for more than 40 years. His works are heart reflections of himself, as well as many other Chinese scholars who are like him, living through and surviving the traumatic movements in China—a witness to the massive economic and social transformations in the past half a century.

Zhao's recent poetry collection *Pains* differs from his previous works. With a more centralized theme in one collection of poems, he tends to offer an internalized experience with his subjects.

The book is consisted of 51 short poems, including "Spine," "Tongue," "The Sole and the Road," "Scars," "Hair," "Nails," "Vocal Cords," "Lacrimal Gland," etc. From the titles of the poems, we can see many of the subjects are about our body organs. Through the subtle observation to the changes of the body parts, we get to realize how we are conquered by time. From being in our prime to falling into decay, we are torn between the unrepeatable birth and a yet-to-come death.

箫

我是一管箫
钻八个孔
我的体内蕴着无数声音
我的前身是 山野幽篁
让
湍激的流水
倒映我迎风摇曳的绿影

等待你的唇舌
等待你温柔而
激越的气息
穿越我的身体
来吧，你的
温暖的手指
逐一按我的
笛孔   洞

如泣如诉

穿越
等待你的呼吸
走我的身体
走每一个洞口徘徊

Bamboo Flute, see page 48.

108

In modern poetry, the "body" is always connected with happiness and desires, which has nothing to do with movements and politics. However, in *Pains*, we read of a body that begins to face its aging self with Montaigne-like musings and contemplation.

If Zhao's poetry in the past decades feature a distinctive brightness and grandeur of the Chinese landscape, like what we often read in Chinese translation of Pushkin's poems, here after sixty years of age, this later work of Zhao Lihong turns to the inside—an undoubted gaze to confront the uneasiness, the obscure and the fractured self.

There is a popular piece of prose by Zhao, titled "Poetic Sentiment," which was once selected for middle school reading curriculum. In the article, Zhao says "Poetic sentiment is an emotion that any living soul can discover or create in this lively world. Words and phrases that rhyme with verse are not necessary. We could all be poets, so long as we wave our soul's flag high above the vast expanse of the land; we laugh, cry, thump and sign truly and freely with echoes heard from the crowd; and we feel our heart's cord shivering for love's calling..."

From this paragraph, we read of a pure romanticism in poetry writing, which emphasizes on passion, confidence and trust in an expression of words. However, in *Pains* all these have disappeared:

> I am harassed by pain, frequently
> but I am not afraid
>
> —"Pains"

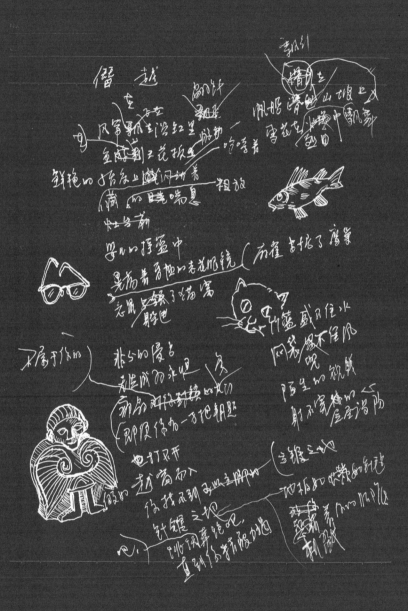

Trespassing, see page 62.

The passion to capture or feel for the outside world is replaced by some limited and concrete sensibility of the body—the pains, sharp in the flesh. So to speak, body pains have made the poet reconsider the poetic sentiment he once adopted. From bravely embracing the world outside, he now has turned to care for his inner self—a return to the classical approach to the study of poetry. However, he has yet to lament like a classicist who looks to the death of an individual with a sober and solemn mind, hasn't lost all his hopes.

They are worried eyes
are pains poised to permeate
In every scar
wings will be born
—"Scars"

As he sets his eyes from the outside to the solid pains within himself, he sees new possibilities as the past on which his career is founded suddenly collapsed. But he is no longer eager to find the answers. Instead, he works deliberately to record the changes in process.

I bring my feet over the threshold
and walk into three spaces at once
—"Walking into Three Spaces at Once"

As his body suffers the pains, his soul wanders back while his soul travels to the future. Such kind of split can be felt from time to time as one reads between the lines throughout *Pains*, which features a hesitant and obscure voice wailing for the ailing body parts.

At the same time, something new is growing as the pains cause the split, and the spilt dissolve the once complete subject for feelings. Personal sadness and happiness is deserted to be replaced by an observation which shows individuals as being part of the universe that is doomed to failure and annihilation.

walking away from the light
light takes on mass
propelling me forward
           —"Dark Matter"

You hang perpendicular
like a glaringly pure pillar
a burning crystal
or the winter ice
Do you lead to freedom
to a sky where wings unfold
           —"Beam of Light"

Therefore, after the pains are felt by the body, we see light, naturally, becoming the other subject of his poems. To some extent, *Pains* can be seen as a retreat and profound withdrawal in the author's poetic career that has stretched as long as half of his lifetime. It is a reflection of the past and deep thoughts on death. He has invited death into his works, and made every endeavor to collect all he has to be a light to resurrect the dead.

Zhang Dinghao